D0193313

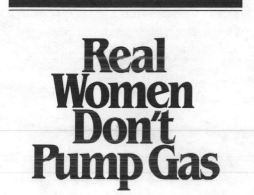

Real Women Don't Pump Gas

This book is dedicated to Queen Isabella of Spain. Without her, the New World, and hence the Pittsburgh Steelers, the Hoover Dam, and Ernest Hemingway, would not have been possible—and Christopher Columbus would have ended up sipping Sangria and eating quiche in Lisbon.

Naturally, he took all the credit.

Real Women Don't Pump Gas

by Joyce Jillson

Illustrated by Lee Lorenz

PUBLISHED BY POCKET BOOKS NEW YORK

Another *Original* publication of POCKET BOOKS

POCKET BOOKS, a Simon & Schuster division of
GULF & WESTERN CORPORATION
POCKET 1230 Avenue of the Americas, New York, N.Y. 10020

Text Copyright © 1982 by Joyce Jillson
Illustrations and other material Copyright © 1982 by Pocket Books,
a Simon & Schuster division of Gulf & Western Corporation

ISBN: 0-671-46309-8

First Pocket Books printing December, 1982

10 9 8 7 6 5 4 3 2 1

Design by Jacques Chazaud

Contents

Author's Note

Bruce Feirstein is essentially correct when he says "Real Men don't eat quiche."

A man could not possibly appreciate this subtle blend of cream, eggs, herbs, and spices, which represents the epitome of refined civilization.

Real Women are secure enough to cook, serve, and eat whatever they damn well please.

Bruce: Do us all a favor and stick to fixing transmissions.

1
Introduction

*T*hings have gotten out of control.
For the past year all we've been hearing about is Real Men. Real Men's clothing. Real Men's reading. Real Men's dining choices (if you consider the manner in which Real Men eat to be dining, rather than something resembling a mass feeding at the zoo).

The problem, however, is that in the midst of all this strutting about inventing the chain saw, municipal bonds, and oral sex, everyone has overlooked one important fact:

Who do you think brought all those Real Men into the world in the first place?

Who carried them for nine months?

Who cooked their first hamburgers?

Who taught them how to open a bottle of ketchup?

Real Women, of course.

Going a step further, let us not forget that even the pope has a mother, Clint Eastwood did not spring whole from the loins of a man, and throughout history we have always referred to the planet as Mother Earth, and the environment as Mother Nature.

(Not to mention the fact that the greatest enemy known to man has always been known as Father Time.)

But the problem today is larger than just Real Men.

The problem is that too many women want to be Real Men—instead of Real Women.

In the old days, for example, Ingrid Bergman knew she was beautiful and managed to traipse all over the world as an independent woman in *Casablanca* without thinking that her brains or independence compromised her sex appeal.

But let's face it—aren't we all just a little bit tired of Meryl Streep apologizing for her beauty?

Or Jill Clayburgh, Sandy Dennis, Diane Keaton, and Mary Steenburgen confusing their neuroses with sex appeal?

This book is designed to distinguish Real Women from those who aren't. It's the complete guide to surviving in an age of house husbands, "chairpersons," and television commercials saying it's okay to invite a man over for Harveys Bristol Cream—when we all know that if he truly was a Real Man, *he* would have called you in the first place.

Thus, read on. And with luck we may return to the age of Bette Davis, Lauren Bacall, and Calvin Coolidge—when Mrs. Coolidge was running the country.

Real Women
Quiz #1

Q. What's a Real Woman's idea of successful foreplay?

A. Flowers, dinner, and a movie.

2

The Modern Real Woman

Jennifer guided her sleek graphite Audi 5000 up to the self-service pump at the local Exxon station. It was 7:30 a.m. She had just finished an hour's workout on the Nautilus machine and was on her way into Manhattan to take part in the dismembering of Braniff—an airline that was run into the ground by "Real Men."

"I'll get the gas," said her partner, Kristin, opening the passenger door.

"You'll do no such thing," Jennifer shot back, grabbing her arm and pulling her back into the car. "The time has come to draw the line. And the line, which we don't cross, is at self-service gas stations. It's time to return to the days of femininity. We can run the whole damn oil company—but we're not pumping the gas. If we wait long enough, some big lug will think that we're helpless girls and will pump the junk *for* us."

Kristin looked at her quizzically. Was this really the senior partner of Wall Street's biggest law firm speaking? A woman who had arranged the breakup of A.T.& T., put her husband through medical school, and could also bake the best quiche west of Paris in less than three minutes flat?

As the cars began to back up and honk behind her, Jennifer remained calm.

"Listen," she continued, "the truth is that it's time to become feminine again. I'm sick of carrying a bigger briefcase than the men in my office to prove that I'm one of the boys. I'm tired of playing dumb about football in order to make men feel superior at Monday morning meetings. If I were calling the plays, the Giants would have made the Super Bowl years ago."

By now there were hundreds of cars backed up onto the street. Kristin was starting to sweat.

"Are you sure you don't want me to pump the gas?"

"Don't you understand?" Jennifer continued, undaunted. "Real Women are afraid to be themselves today. Every bastion of femininity is being taken away. Do you realize that the blow dryer was created for women, and yet men are now carrying them in their cars for touch-ups? And what about cologne? It used to be our secret weapon. But now you can't go on a date without checking to see that your colognes are compatible first."

As the crowd of cars grew outside Jennifer's window, a policeman approached.

"I mean look at it this way. Was Lana Turner discovered at a gas pump? Did Jack Kennedy fall in love with a woman who had just used a dipstick to check her oil? Do you think Elizabeth Taylor has any idea where the gas tank *is*?

"Of course not. And that's exactly the point. Who are our heroines today? Jill Clayburgh? Meryl Streep? Bella Abzug? Women who continually have men leave them, apologize for their looks, and wear strange hats?"

"Thank goodness for the Rockettes, Linda Evans, Kate Hepburn, and Miss Piggy. Real Women, every last one. Women who wouldn't pump gas—and don't have to continually prove that they're men's equals—when in fact they *know* they're superior."

The policeman knocked on her window. Kristin was mortified. "I think he's going to arrest us," she whispered.

"Just leave this to me," Jennifer replied, lowering the car window.

"Excuse me, ma'am, but is there some problem?" the policeman asked.

"Yes," she responded in her most self-assured voice. "We'll have five dollars of regular, please."

As he filled the tank Jennifer smiled at Kristin. "You see? Anything's possible for a Real Woman."

"Excuse me," the policeman interrupted. "Will there be anything else?"

Kristin cleared her throat. "Yes. Would you mind checking the oil?"

3
The Real Woman's Credo

You can't be too rich, too thin, or have too many silk blouses.

4

*Who's Who in
Real Women*

To be today's Real Woman, you need to have the physique of Venus, the cunning of Cleopatra, the courage of Joan of Arc, the wardrobe of Marie Antoinette, and the cleaning ability of Ammonia D.

When you see Marlo Thomas, Lee Grant, and Valerie Harper pumping gas, you know they obviously have the money to go to the full-service island but apparently feel that doing it themselves makes a meaningful social statement.

And Gloria Steinem? She'd set up a woman's cooperative garage.

Nancy Reagan is a Real Woman. Not because she's the President's wife, but because she has had the good fortune to find a hairdresser who is content NEVER to change her hairstyle.

Real Women know that Coco Chanel, the Duchess of Windsor, Dorothy Parker, and Judy Garland would never have pumped gas—that's what underlings and press agents are for.

Can you imagine Jackie Onassis, Lady Bird Johnson, Princess Diana, or Joan Ludden getting out of their limousines and filling them with gas?

But now think about Ellen Burstyn or Shana Alexander. Wouldn't they be right at home topping off the tank of their four-wheel drives?

Barbara Bush is a Real Woman. Barbara will not dye her snowy locks just to make V.P. George look younger. That's a Real Woman. A Real Woman always, always has one silly little issue that she'll refuse to budge on. (It is often that silly little issue that leads to divorce.)

Secretaries are Real Women. All too often.

Real Women do not want to look like Jane Fonda. Real Women know that putting your leg up to your head is no way to pose for the cover of a book.

Real Women know that being Miss America is better than being a consumer advocate. That's why, although she qualified once, Bess Myerson is no longer a Real Woman.

Only a Real Woman like Jeane Kirkpatrick could get Alexander Haig out of the State Department.

Lynn Redgrave pumps gas and feeds her baby at the same time.

Jacki Sorensen, Mary Kay, and Estee Lauder are all Real Women. Real Women are secure enough to help other women look good.

Texas women can pump gas, but ONLY if the crude comes from their very own well.

Annette Funicello will always be a Real Woman.

Mrs. Frank Sinatra pumps gas HER WAY, but there's no question in anyone's mind that she's a Real Woman.

The list goes on, but in summation, Real Women don't want Burt Reynolds. They want Steven Spielberg. No Real Woman gets turned on by a man driving two hundred miles per hour. But she'd gladly give her heart to someone who can make millions of Real Men cry.

To guide your own search for Real Women, here are some more examples:

Real Women

Princess Diana
Nancy Drew
Lena Horne
Greta Garbo
Marilyn Monroe
Alice Cramden
Nancy Kissinger
Bill Agee
Dolly Parton
The Lennon Sisters
Jacqueline Susann
Ann-Margret
Helen Gurley Brown
Jackie Bisset
Ed Asner
Raquel Welch
Justice Sandra Day O'Connor
Elizabeth Taylor
Eleanor Roosevelt
Betty Crocker
Dr. Ruth Westheimer
Lassie

The Gas Pumpers

Ethel Mertz
Dr. Joyce Brothers
Princess Caroline
Debbie Reynolds
Princess Anne
Glenda Jackson
Teri Shields
Faye Dunaway
Susan Sarandon
Lucy Van Pelt
Vanessa Redgrave
Wayne Newton
Pauline Kael
Linda McCartney

Women Who Think They're Real Women but Try Too Hard

Mary Cunningham
Suzanne Somers
Diane Keaton
Liza Minnelli
Diane Von Furstenberg
Margaret Trudeau
Cher
Charo (Real Women have two names)
Xaviera Hollander
Shere Hite

Real Woman Quiz #2

1. Have you worn panty hose with runs in them under a pair of pants?

2. Does the dry cleaner know your name and telephone number by heart?

3. On vacation, do you worry about being away from your plants?

4. Have you been keeping track of exactly where the killer bees are, and do you know what their expected arrival time is in your part of the country?

5. Did you cry when Prince Charles got engaged?

6. Do you know the date of your cat's or dog's birthday?

7. Are ten pounds (either losing them or gaining them) all that stand between you and physical perfection?

If you answered yes to all 7 questions, congratulations, you're a Real Woman. If you answered yes to 6–4, you've probably lifted the hood of your car. If you answered yes to 3 or less, you've probably lifted the car.

MRS. J. FINKL & DAUGHTER-IN-LAW
(FORMERLY J. FINKL & SON)

Bloodiest takeover struggle I ever witnessed.

5

The Working Real Woman

Real Women know that equality doesn't mean that a woman *has* to work. The Real Woman believes that in life—as in high school—there should be electives. The working Real Woman has a double dilemma—she not only has to work forty hours a week, but she has to prove to outsiders that in the process she's not cheating her family.

Real Women who work are some of the best actresses in the world. They go around giving orders and being decisive all day long; then they go out to dinner and have to pretend it is really helpful when a date interprets their order so the maitre d' can understand it.

Real Women network, but they do not refer to their best friends or relatives as contacts.

In a Real Woman's office you will not see a desk. She will have a table. And there won't be a sign on it saying "The buck stops here." Real Women know the buck stops at Bloomingdale's.

Real Women secretaries show their decorating talents at their desks. How? Real Women secretaries have plants, pretty pencil holders, gingham-covered picture frames, and flowers, either real or fake, on or in something. It is the Real Woman secretary who circulates the get-well and condolence cards throughout the office so everyone can sign. Although just about everyone makes more than she does, the Real Woman secretary will still get stuck paying for this.

You won't find our Real Woman in a tailored, mannish business suit. One reason she works is to buy pretty clothes. Wearing those sexless uniforms would defeat the whole purpose of her climb to success.

Jobs Held by Real Women vs.
Jobs Held by Gas Pumpers

Pet shop owner *vs.* Stunt woman

Talk show hostess *vs.* Sells sex aids at home

Marine biologist *vs.* Oil rig operator

Secretary *vs.* Union organizer

Vice-president of *vs.* Comptroller of
a company   a company

Flight attendant *vs.* Air cargo pilot

Advertising copywriter *vs.* Lobbyist for the P.L.O.

Weathergirl *vs.* Astronaut

Beautician *vs.* Mortician

Receptionist *vs.* Mud wrestler

Vista volunteer *vs.* Alaska pipeline worker

Data processor *vs.* Credit bureau executive

Mistress *vs.* Palimony petitioner

Fashion editor *vs.* Detective

Stockbroker *vs.* Commodities trader

Ice-skating *vs.* Professional
champion   hockey player

Home economics teacher *vs.* Sanitation worker

Singer *vs.* Sound engineer

Anchorwoman *vs.* A merchant marine

6

The Real Woman and Her Money

A Real Woman has a special attitude toward money. If she earns it, it is hers; if her husband earns it, it is theirs.

A Real Woman has two sets of credit cards: one in her maiden name and one in her husband's name. She uses only the ones in her husband's name, keeping her old cards as her special security blanket.

A Real Woman is 100 percent different from a man: She would never stay in a job (although she would stay in a marriage) just because of the pension plan.

Although a Real Woman contributes to the household expenses, she wants to buy luxuries, not necessities. A Real Woman wants to pay for the new living room furniture, camp for the kids, and extra clothes, but it is her husband's responsibility to buy her panty hose, since that is a necessity. Real Women do not pay for a man's hair transplants, sex therapy, or gifts for her stepchildren; if a Real Woman pays for these things, she also pays for the divorce.

Real Women are so trusting that they accept the statements sent out by the bank. Real Women believe that having more than a ten-dollar average monthly balance is bad economics. They always need immediate credit and are not ashamed to bounce checks. If a Real Woman bounces more checks than she can afford, she simply closes her account.

I'm afraid the bank can't do anything for you, Miss Trelane, but I'd personally be happy to lend you fifty till payday.

7

Beauty and the Real Woman

Three thousand years after the first woman applied the first eyeliner, Real Women are still seeking the ultimate way to thicken their lashes. In their sincere quest for beauty, they have allowed the cosmetics and fragrance industries to manipulate these simple desires at their expense. This should set the record straight:

Real Women do not wear makeup whose advertisements stress that it's perfect to be worn at a country estate. The Real Woman is not fooled by the ads (with the model, posing in front of a Newport mansion, wearing Royal Delight lipstick) suggesting that rich folk will accept you only if you are wearing this particular lip color. Real Women know that rich folk judge you by your shoes and whether or not you are incorporated in Delaware.

Real Women don't belong to the Junior League, because they're playing with the big boys now. Real Women used to care about being in the Social Register, but no more. Now they are proud of their own accomplishments, not their pedigree. So they don't want beauty ads to refer to them as thoroughbreds, blue bloods, gentry, socialites, or aristocrats. Why is the cosmetics industry trying to foster such class consciousness, the Real Woman wonders?

The Real Woman is secure enough to throw her Ultima II in with the cosmetics she bought at Woolworth's because it's not how much the product costs, it's how skillfully you apply it.

And yes, the Real Woman cares about the environment; but still, she selects feminine care products because they work, not because someone came up with the idea to make them biodegradable.

And a word about fragrances: The Real Woman knows exactly what a fragrance can do and doesn't expect more of it. She doesn't "enter a fragrance" or think it will transport her to the Left Bank of the Seine.

A Real Woman doesn't wear perfume with a name a normal person would have trouble pronouncing. She doesn't buy a scent because the bottle has pretensions of being Waterford. Real Women believe that if an atomizer of cologne is photographed to resemble the opening sequence of *2001*, it probably stinks to the ends of the earth.

As for the perfumes themselves, the Real Woman doesn't buy Scoundrel. Why wear a scent that might encourage a man to be the opposite of what you want him to be? Naturally she'd avoid Tramp with a ten-foot pole.

And if Cie is me, as Candy Bergen asserts, then why would she want to peddle something *that* personal? As for the Charlie fragrance, the Real Woman would like to see how the Charlie model looks the next morning, after she's been pawed by every man in the lobby of the Plaza Hotel.

The Real Woman feels that she's been personally assaulted when department store personnel spray her with a strange perfume, and she hates those little smelly packets that arrive with her charge account bills; they pollute the whole house.

What perfume does the Real Woman wear? Joy, Chanel No. 5, My Sin, Norell—whatever she can't afford. Or whatever her mother gave her for her birthday.

I think we'll both have the businesswoman's lunch—
three whiskey sours and a strawberry yogurt.

Real Woman Quiz #3

Q. How many Real Women does it take to change a light bulb?

A. None. Real Women don't try to change light bulbs. They accept them for what they are.

8. The Real Woman

Real Women know that there are certain hours of the day when their feet automatically take them to the icebox.

10:00 a.m. The results of not eating breakfast set in. The Real Woman eats a candy bar.

3:00 p.m. The results of not eating lunch, because she ate the candy bar, set in. The Real Woman orders out for a double cheeseburger and a Tab.

5:00 p.m. The Real Woman realizes she's blown a whole day of dieting. This self-hatred drives her to the freezer for chocolate chip ice cream.

9:00 p.m. The Real Woman munches a celery stalk, showing admirable self-control. She decides to rearrange the refrigerator.

Diet Clock

11:00 p.m. The Real Woman prepares a low-calorie lunch to take to the office and absentmindedly eats it during the 11:00 news.

1:00 a.m. Since the Real Woman knows that eating before bedtime multiplies the harm a calorie can do, she stays up to watch the late movie.

3:00 a.m. To put herself to sleep, the Real Woman drinks a big glass of skim milk.

7:30 a.m. When she makes her coffee, the Real Woman realizes that the previous night she didn't drink the skim milk, she drank the half-and-half. The Real Woman decides to skip breakfast. A new day begins.

Just give me a Halston wardrobe, a Sassoon hairdo, and Ted Turner's phone number. I'll take it from there.

9

*The Real Woman
Goes Swimming*

Although inch for inch it is probably one of the smallest items in the Real Woman wardrobe, the bathing suit causes more consternation, sweaty palms, and self-criticism—not to mention fear—than any other garment. Before the Real Woman can get excited about a trip to the Caribbean or a summer at a beach cottage, she must think the unthinkable:

"What do my thighs look like?"

"How long can I hold in my stomach muscles this year?"

But with all the styles becoming skimpier and skimpier, the years, kind as they have been to her, have taken their toll. Thus, the Real Woman does not choose her bathing suit, It chooses her.

And so the Real Woman goes to shop.

Here we are able to separate the Real Women from the fakes. A Real Woman never, ever takes her husband or boyfriend along when shopping for a bathing suit.

And for good reason—the lights in those tiny cubicles make her tummy bulge and her untanned skin look pallid. And she cannot lose ten pounds in five seconds, which is the time it takes for a Real Woman to put on the suit and realize that she must diet.

It's a little-known fact that the Real Woman commits a misdemeanor every time she tries on a bathing suit. How? Come on now! How many real Real Women have followed the letter of the law and left their panties on when trying on a latex suit? Wouldn't that defeat the whole purpose of seeing how you would look in this overpriced piece of elastic? And the Real Woman raises one other question: What ever happened to padded bras? She wouldn't use one, of course, but she's just curious.

The Real Woman is a total optimist. She knows that the suit doesn't fit perfectly, but she buys it anyway, thinking that the prospect of having others see her in it—in her present condition—will shame her into dieting.

Between five and seven days before she leaves for her Waterloo, the Real Woman makes these determinations:

How important is swimming anyway?

Does anyone look good in a bathing cap?

And if at this point she has not lost one ounce, the Real Woman decides that she will not go in the water—this summer.

After purchasing all the beach cover-ups at the hotel gift shop, the Real Woman will have a passion for antiquing or anything that gives her a valid excuse to keep away from the water. Next year, she vows, things will be different.

10

A Few Things a Real Woman Carries in Her Purse

Dog-eared address book
Loose telephone numbers
Tissues
Last month's parking receipt
Comb
Pad and pencil
One crayon
Checkbook
Birth control device and back-up device
Grocery list
Nail polish
Sunglasses
Peds
Wallet
Snapshot of friend

Two change purses, one containing
    emergency money ($1.00)
Travel brochure
Aspirin
Credit slip from Sears
One false nail
One loose key
Cologne
Contact lens case
Two-week-old pay stub
Throat lozenges
Credit cards
Dry cleaning tickets
Brush
Child's shoelace
Resume
Vitamin C
Thirty-five-cent coupon
    for breakfast cereal
Emery board
Life Savers
Sanitary napkins
Binaca
Confidential credit report
Makeup remover
Seven paper clips
Magazine instructions for exercises
    you can perform at desk
One earring
Little flashlight with siren
Small food scale
Silhouette Romance

11

One Thing a Real Woman Never Carries in Her Purse

Cash

12

*Five Examples
of People Who
Don't Know What a
Real Woman Is*

1. *The window dressers at Saks Fifth Avenue.* Any woman who stood the way those dummies do to make the clothes look good would have a slipped disc within hours. Real Women know that if you must spend more money on accessories for a dress than on the dress itself, you've bought the wrong dress.

2. *The editors of* Mademoiselle. The Real Woman does not completely redo her wardrobe for every season. She requires only one thing from a winter coat: that it be longer than her dresses. Real Women know that wearing yellow or pink eyeshadow is only for punk rockers. Real Women know that being a guest editor for *Mademoiselle* doesn't qualify you for anything—except the Junior League.

3. *The automobile industry.* If those Detroit biggies knew how important it was for a Real Woman to have a magnifying mirror on her car's visor, they'd advertise that instead of turbo engines.

4. *Bathing suit manufacturers.* Any Real Woman worth her salt has a different size top than bottom. This forces the Real Woman to be deceptive and try to palm off a size eight top and a size twelve bottom as a matched set at the check-out counter.

5. *Hugh Hefner.*

13

*Real Woman
Movie Stars*

Real Women have very strong opinions about whom they like to see on the silver screen.

The Real Woman will not spend money to see Ryan O'Neal, James Coburn, or Robert De Niro (no matter how good an actor he is) show off their muscles. And they've seen enough of Robin Williams, Henry Winkler, and Alan Alda to know they not only lack muscles, but they look most manly on a small screen.

The Real Woman will not pay good money to see John Travolta unless she is sure he will dance.

The Real Woman does not like George Segal or Richard Harris. It has nothing to do with being a Real Woman though. No one likes them.

Cary Grant is the Real Woman's hero. Why did he have to retire from films, when the old actors who should have bowed out gracefully continue to go on—year after year—playing World War II generals?

Real Women are also disillusioned with Meryl Streep. Only Meryl could make a Real Woman believe that Dustin Hoffman deserved the kid.

And a word about Marsha Mason. Real Women like to see her movies because Marsha's the only female star their husbands don't want to go to bed with.

Barbra Streisand is a Real Woman. Only a Real Woman would elevate her hairdresser to boyfriend and then make him a producer too. Why? Because Real Women know how important a good haircut is, and secondly, once they have found it, they don't want anyone else to have it.

Marilyn Monroe was the ultimate Real Woman Movie Star.

Here are the movies a Real Woman will spend her hard-earned cash on:

Singin' in the Rain
Gigi
Gone with the Wind
An Officer and a Gentleman
Funny Girl
National Velvet
King Kong
How to Marry a Millionaire
The Way We Were
Wuthering Heights
The Red Shoes
A Star Is Born (any version)
Where the Boys Are

14

Great Lines from Real Woman Movies

"La-de-da."
—Diane Keaton in *Annie Hall*

15

More Great Lines from Real Woman Movies

"Ohhh . . . Superman."
　　—Margot Kidder in *Superman*

I respect you as a person, Jonathan, but I'm afraid you don't address my needs as a person.

16

Real Woman Magazines

The Real Woman reads *Glamour, House Beautiful, Paris-Match,* and *Cosmopolitan.* Lately, though, she wonders if she wants to be "that *Cosmopolitan* girl." Here are these stunning women who look like models and think like Margaret Thatcher and what happens to them (according to the articles)? They end up in relationships with married men. This is good advice?

The Real Woman will only buy *Town & Country* when she's at an airport gift shop. Otherwise she feels too bad seeing rich people with tax shelters riding to the hounds when her budget is going to the dogs.

The Real Woman has subscribed to *Scientific American* but she prefers *Psychology Today.* The Real Woman is a pragmatist. She doesn't want to learn the game theory behind backgammon, she simply wants to psyche out her opponent.

The Real Woman got *Playgirl* a few times. She tried to like it, but she's sick of seeing men in the same three poses:

(1) coming out of the shower dripping wet;

(2) laying on their side, one arm draped over their crotches, and a bent arm holding up their heads; and

(3) unbuttoning a pair of jeans. Can't men do anything else? Besides, with *Playgirl* no one would believe you bought it for the articles.

And *Sports Illustrated?* Not on your life. The only thing the Real Woman missed by not reading this was that for three years, she didn't know who Christie Brinkley was.

17

The Real Woman's Library

Non-fiction

Everything by Judith Krantz
Everything by Jacqueline Susann
Romeo and Juliet

Fiction

How to Make Love to a Man
The Beverly Hills Diet
Shelley
How to Be Your Own Best Friend
Living Alone and Liking It
Dress for Success
The G-Spot
Neiman-Marcus catalog
Thin Thighs in 30 Days
Real Men Don't Eat Quiche

18

Real Moms

Only a Real Woman can turn herself into a Real Mom. We used to have lots of role models for these unselfish creatures, but now only Donna Reed and Harriet Nelson come to mind. In today's television programs the mothers seem to have more problems than the kids. Just watch any episode of *Family Feud* and you wonder how the teenagers are going to live through their parents' second adolescence.

Since Real Moms are almost extinct, here's how to spot this one-in-a-million phenomenon:

Real Moms do volunteer work.

Real Moms wear corsages.

Real Moms believe in nepotism.

Real Moms fix their teenage daughters up with a second cousin when they don't have a date for the prom.

Real Moms have ESP and know when their children are in trouble.

Real Moms like the suburbs. They decorate their homes for the holidays. In fact, a true Real Mom will stay up all night before Christmas putting the trains together and doing the last-minute wrapping, cooking, and baking. A Real Mom always wishes she had more money to spend on her children.

Real Moms wear earrings during the day. They make pudding when you are sick. And they taste the cough syrup themselves before they make you take it. Real Moms always have milk of magnesia handy. They swear that Mercurochrome doesn't sting.

A Real Mom will go through the trash when a kid announces that he "thinks he threw his bite plate in the wastepaper basket."

Despair hits the Real Mom when her children need her to help with their science fair projects. She doesn't know what to do, except—of course—to turn her stove and refrigerator over to budding scientists who make her kitchen smell like a fish tank. So a Real Mom will end up doing the lettering for the posters.

Real Moms have the good sense to put a lock on their bedroom door. Gas-pumping parents call having the door ajar "sharing."

Gas pumpers judge a man by how much he tips the baby sitter.

Real Moms don't make mother-in-law jokes. They know that if it weren't for their in-laws, they'd never have gotten the down payment to buy a house. And a further point: Real Moms know kids should be raised in houses, not condos.

Real Moms are never allergic to anything their children like. A real Real Mom will live with a cat that makes her sneeze for ten years. But if anyone suggests that her new, prized, expensive sectional sofa could make one of her children tear, for an instant, it would be on its way to Goodwill within the hour.

Real Moms like mother-and-daughter outfits.

Gas pumpers dress their four-year-old daughters in designer clothes, believing that if they're outfitted as adults they'll suddenly act like them—and be no more trouble. No Real Mom would buy a peignoir set for a little girl.

Real Moms name their children after foods and flowers: Muffin, Daisy, Berry, and Rose. They do not name their offspring after counties in Ireland: Courtney, Kimberly, Clare, Shannon, or Kerry.

And finally, Real Moms spank their kids, but it hurts *them* more.

19
Great Moments in Real Woman Literature #1

"Which one of you bitches is my mother?"

—*Lace* by Shirley Conran

20

The
Real Woman
Driver

If ever there were a symbol for the modern Real Woman, it is the automobile—to be more specific, the hatchback. These cars got Real Women into the mainstream of life as well as back and forth to the grocery with the least amount of effort.

Real Women buy five dollars' worth of gasoline at a time. Gas pumpers always fill up. (Wouldn't you after going through all that mess?)

Real Women do not drive stick shifts. Gas pumpers switch from second to third and back to second with the ease of a truck driver. Real Women do not drive with one headlight or pass on the right. They don't want mag wheels.

To some Real Women a car is a home away from home. Real Women who work consider their car's trunk to be an all-purpose office. They would never be caught without tissues in the glove compartment.

The hobby of a Real Woman is locking herself out of her car. So now she carries a clothes hanger but forgets that she can't get to the hanger if this happens and so feels very secure.

Gas pumpers care about the fuel injector system working properly. Real Women know that if the car moves it's obviously okay. If a Real Woman hears a funny sound and doesn't have time to stop at a gas station, she just turns the radio up loud to cover the sound and relieve her worries.

How does the Real Woman select a car? By name. Here are some of her feminine guidelines:

Real Women do not drive cars named after living things that can eat or bite them. They do not drive Cougars, Jaguars, Barracudas, Skyhawks, Spiders, Bugs, Stingrays, Phoenixes, or Cobras.

They drive cars named after friendly animals: Rabbits, Pintos, Colts, Impalas, and Mustangs. To this day a pink Mustang remains the epitome of the Real Woman car. All Impalas and Mustangs bring back fond teenage memories for the Real Woman. Mercedes do not. Whoever heard of a girl getting pinned in a Mercedes? (My apologies to Beverly Hills High School graduates.)

Real Women also buy cars named after places they would like to visit: Monte Carlo, Biarritz, Seville, Cordoba, Capri, Malibu, and certainly Grand Prix.

Forget a Plymouth or a Pontiac. And a Dodge? That's what a Real Woman *does* while driving, not what she sits in.

A Real Woman wants a man to buy a convertible or a car with a sun roof. But she will always complain when he puts the top down, because the wind is ruining her hair.

And finally . . . Real Women will not lease a car. They don't even believe in financing it. Real Women want a Real Man to buy it outright.

In addition, your Honor, I'd like to point out that my client has never known the love of a good woman.

21

The Real Woman's Musical History

Wouldn't It Be Nice

It Must Be Him

My Guy

It's My Party

Here Comes the Bride

Crying in the Chapel

Tears on My Pillow

You're So Vain

Now It's Judy's Turn to Cry

99 Tears

Cry Me a River

Don't Cry Out Loud

I'm Gonna Wash That Man Right Out of My Hair

Alone Again, Naturally

The Second Time Around

Wouldn't It Be Nice

Real Woman Quiz #4

Q. What does a Real Woman say about Gloria Steinem?

A. Gloria who?

Well, so long. You've been terribly sweet, and if I ever get carried off by a dragon again, I'll certainly give you a holler.

22. The Real Woman's

	Monday	Tuesday	Wednesday
9:00	Donahue	Donahue	Donahue
9:30			
10:00	The Richard Simmons Show	The Richard Simmons Show	The Richard Simmons Show
10:30			
11:00	General Hospital	General Hospital	General Hospital
11:30			
12:00	Happy Days	The Dating Game	Mary Hartman, Mary Hartman
12:30		The Newlywed Game	
1:00	Let's Make a Deal	Family Feud	Family
1:30			Rhoda
2:00	I Dream of Jeannie	"A Summer Place"	
2:30	The Big Payoff		That Girl
3:00	Green Acres		I Love Lucy
3:30	Petticoat Junction		
4:00	Peyton Place	Lou Grant	"Rebecca"
4:30			
5:00	Dark Shadows	Merv Griffin	
5:30			
6:00	News with Walter Cronkite	News with Walter Cronkite	News with Walter Cronkite
6:30			
7:00	Carol Burnett	Dinah!	Dr. Kildare
7:30			
8:00	The Grammy Awards	Miss America Pageant	Miss Universe Pageant

Television Utopia

Thursday	Friday	Saturday	Sunday	
Donahue	Donahue		"The Little Princess"	
The Richard Simmons Show	The Richard Simmons Show	Sesame Street		
General Hospital	General Hospital		Leave It to Beaver	
Father Knows Best		Queen for a Day		
Julia Child	"An Affair to Remember"		Fantasy Island	
		Laverne & Shirley		
"White Christmas"	The Galloping Gourmet	American Bandstand	"Gidget Goes Hawaiian"	
Bewitched	"Pillow Talk"			
Little House on the Prairie		"Love Is a Many Splendored Thing"	"The Bad and the Beautiful"	
Mary Tyler Moore	The Patty Duke Show			
News with Walter Cronkite	News with Walter Cronkite	Wide World of Sports: Ice Skating Championship Gymnastics Championship	M*A*S*H	
Trapper John, M.D.	Mission: Impossible		60 Minutes	
Country Music Awards	The Tony Awards	Academy Awards	Upstairs, Downstairs	

23

How to Spot a Real Woman at a Party

A Real Woman brings a hostess gift.

A Real Woman is able to eat an hors d'oeuvre while juggling a drink, her purse, and a cigarette in her free hand.

A Real Woman does not complain to the other guests that she has a headache—that's her date's problem.

A Real Woman won't be thrilled when the host announces that he has "special" movies to show on his home video equipment.

At a big gathering the Real Woman will not be seen carrying the flower arrangements home.

Real Women do not tell dirty jokes, though they may laugh at them.

Real Women who wear slinky dresses are able to hold their stomachs in all night.

When a Real Woman visits the bathroom, she'll come out with powder on her nose, not in it.

If a Real Woman is pushed into the pool during these frivolities, the first thing she will worry about is her hair. Gas pumpers worry that their digital watches will be ruined.

My politics are simple—peace through strength, strength through joy, and joy through sex.

Real Woman Drinks

Kir
Strawberry daiquiri
Vodka gimlet
Whiskey sour
Mai Tai
Brandy Alexander
Kahlua
Tia Maria
Red Russian
Black Russian
White Russian
Vermouth
Vermouth Cassis
Mint Julep
Mimosa
Dubonnet Fizz
Piña Colada
Velvet Hammer
Spritzer
Singapore Sling
Stinger
Planter's Punch
Joe Rose

Any drink in which a straw can stand by itself

Gas Pumper's Drink

Stolichnaya straight

24

What the Real Woman Wants in a Man

As the Real Woman moves through life, her requirements regarding men change. Based on age, here are some of the important essentials:

Age 20: Good looks. Marvelous sense of humor. Education, preferably Harvard Law. Athletic ability. Family money. Similar political beliefs. Interest in travel. Appreciation of the arts. Neat. Able to cook for himself. Good dresser. Punctual. Not overly perfectionistic. Comfortable around the Real Woman's family and girlfriends. Someone who believes in commitment. Similar religious background. Unencumbered by student loans. Good driving record. Moderate drinker; knowledge of wines highly desirable. Ambitious. Likes children. Generous. Excellent communicator.

Goal: Marriage.

Age 30: Someone completely over his ex-wife. Good job with potential. Laughs easily. Into physical fitness. Puts up with children. Drinking problem under control. Enjoys going to the movies. Owns a car. Shares business knowledge.

Goal: To announce her engagement and hopefully marry.

Age 40: Nice. If not good looking at least clean. Reliable. Doesn't fall asleep over dinner. Someone who occasionally watches the evening news.

Goal: Move in together and hopefully marry.

Age 50: Someone who gets over his moods quickly. Clean-smelling breath. His children don't berate her.

Goal: Spend holidays together. Marriage unlikely, but hoped for.

Age 60: Good dentures. Likes her cooking. Changes underwear weekly.

Goal: Certainly not marriage, which would cut her Social Security benefits.

He's not much in bed, but he's always been a good provider.

25

*Dating
the Real Woman*

*I*t's a wonder a Real Woman ever meets someone to marry. But she does, and here's how:

Real Women do not double date.

Real Women do not order anything with onions. Gas pumpers request that the chef put extra garlic into the bouillabaisse.

Real Women do not comment on how good looking the waiter is. Gas pumpers will ask if he's ever appeared at a strip joint.

A Real Woman never splits the check. She can't. A Real Woman never carries money on a date.

Real Women seem game for just about anything—except bed.

You can tell you are in the company of a Real Woman by what she changes into at her apartment. A Real Woman will put on a pastel-colored robe or negligee. A Gas pumper will put on argyle socks, her Hawaiian muu-muu, and a video cassette of *Nightline*.

When a Real Woman entertains a man in her home, she makes sure she has plenty of NoDoz. She's afraid that she'll fall asleep when the man starts recounting his life story and gets to the part about boot camp.

After spending the first night with a man, what does a Real Woman do?

1. She tries to figure out if they should live at his place or hers.

2. She names the children.

3. She plans the shortest route to the bathroom, where her robe is hanging behind the door.

When the Real Woman, after struggling through the dating scene, gets married, she wears white. If it's a second or third or fourth marriage, she describes her dress as off-white, dusty pink, cream, beige, sand, light peach, or buff. But is it? No. The gown is pearly white, as it should be. If the Real Woman is going to defy tradition by paying for her own wedding, she's not going to adhere to some fuddy-duddy dress code. And, it's nice to hand down a wedding gown to a daughter, and with multiple marriages she'll have one for each of them.

26
Great Moments in Real Woman Literature #2

"Oh, I love a pretty house. I care about clothes. I'm not Oriana Fallaci. All the domestic things are very real and important to me. I should be living the life my married friends live. But you know what my daughter says? 'Mummy doesn't drive. Mummy doesn't play games. Mummy burns the meat loaf. My mummy can't do *anything* but television.'"

—Barbara Walters quoting her daughter, Jacqueline, regarding her domesticity. *Cosmopolitan* Magazine, June 1982

27

Sex and the Real Woman

I t used to be so clear for Real Women. They were told to choose a husband who was a good provider. Period. It didn't matter that he didn't know the Kama Sutra or couldn't locate the G-spot. Women wanted a man who was stable and who would be a good father. As for being physically attractive, well, in the good old days the men left that sort of thing up to their wives.

The Real Woman knows she has as much right to make the first move as any man. And she'll be outraged at any suggestion that she shouldn't. But does the Real Woman make the first move? Not on your life. A Real Woman secretly wants to be dominated, and if she has to take those first steps herself, she surely won't respect the man in the morning.

Sex for the Real Woman is not a combat sport, it is more like the Battle of the Network Stars. A lot of play acting and strutting, and everyone has a good time. But you can tell that men see sex as the Super Bowl from the words they use to describe it. In bed men "fumble," "make conquests," "have botched attempts" and "false starts." If they aren't sure if a woman likes them, they "take a shot at it anyway." They "tough it out," "call for half time," and, when things aren't going all that well, they "double fault," "dribble," and tell themselves to "punt."

Separating emotions and sex is impossible for a Real Woman. The proof? The fact that so many Real Woman can only express their anger in bed.

Real Women like to cuddle.

Real Women not only buy sexy nightgowns, but they wear them even after they are married.

Real Women may not always enjoy sex, but they have the courtesy to say they do.

Real Women never tell you when they are faking.

Real Women exclaim—even to the most bumbling fool—that he is absolutely the best. Gas pumpers stop right in the middle of lovemaking, get out of bed, grab a sex manual, and tell a man to read pages 53 to 58 and then get back to her.

Real Women are not sex therapists. And a Real Woman would only suggest a man see one when she is absolutely positive that their relationship has no future.

Real Women do not use sex aids.

When a Real Woman is with her friends, she can finally laugh about the macho inconsideration that made her cry herself to sleep the night before.

The only place a Real Woman can't really enjoy sex is in her parents' house—after she's married. This is ironic because, before she got married, it was the only place she *could*.

Real Women cook breakfast in the morning. Gas pumpers open a can of Tab and ask if you'd like to split it. If a Real Woman stays with a man, she goes home in the morning and not in the middle of the night. She is not ashamed to walk past her apartment manager wearing rhinestones and chiffon at eleven on a Sunday morning.

28. *Great Dates in*

A.D. 68
Mrs. Nero
says she's tired of
playing second
fiddle.

1848
Gold discovered in
California. The
West seems
promising to the
Real Woman, who
decides to become
the first mail-order
bride.

1,000,000 B.C.
Eve discovers the
Beverly Hills diet.

10,000 B.C.
Delilah becomes
the first stand-up
comedienne-barber.
Brings the house
down.

May 19, 1806
Real Woman
Sacajawea,
mad at Lewis and
Clark for calling
her a back-seat
driver, takes them
two months out of
their way for
revenge.

Real Woman History

1885
First obscene
telephone call
made to a Real
Woman.

1937
First
shopping cart
invented.

February 1910
Boy Scouts
formed. A Real
Woman becomes
the first den
mother.

1928
Janet Gaynor
wins the first
Academy Award
for best actress in
the film *Seventh
Heaven.*

1888
Real Woman
decides to hang up
telephone.

1939
First Real Woman
charge account
at Peck and Peck.

Great Dates in Real Woman History

1950
Frozen foods
first sold. Real
Women realize that
this gives them the
free time to pursue
a career.

1961
Johnson &
Johnson
surgical glue
first used by a Real
Woman to apply
false eyelashes.

1953
Real Woman
gets first upright
vacuum cleaner.

1952
First
hydrogen device
exploded in the
Pacific.
By-products of this
create a
faster-acting
hydrogen peroxide
to bleach the Real
Woman's hair.

1960
Real Women
begin
to take oral
contraceptives.

(Continued)

1963
Joan Baez performs at Newport Jazz Festival; Real Women decide not to curl hair for a decade.

1974
Real Women permanently stop taking oral contraceptives.

1972
Real Woman finally returns original shopping cart to grocery store.

1973
Real Woman Joanna Carson convinces husband, Johnny, to stop coloring his hair. White hair becomes sexy.

1965
First pair of panty hose worn by a Real Woman.

1980
Mommie Dearest published.

I call it the Post-Superbowl Syndrome. I think it has something to do with their hormones.

Real Woman Quiz #5

 How many gas pumpers does it take to cross the road?

 Ten. One to suggest it, eight to convene a symposium, and one to write it up in *Ms*.

29. The Real Woman's History

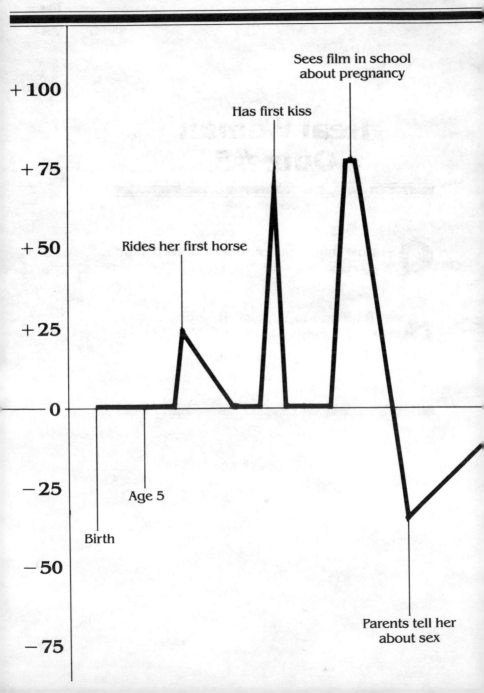

Sees film in school about pregnancy

Has first kiss

Rides her first horse

+100

+75

+50

+25

0

-25

-50

-75

Age 5

Birth

Parents tell her about sex

# of Sexual Satisfaction

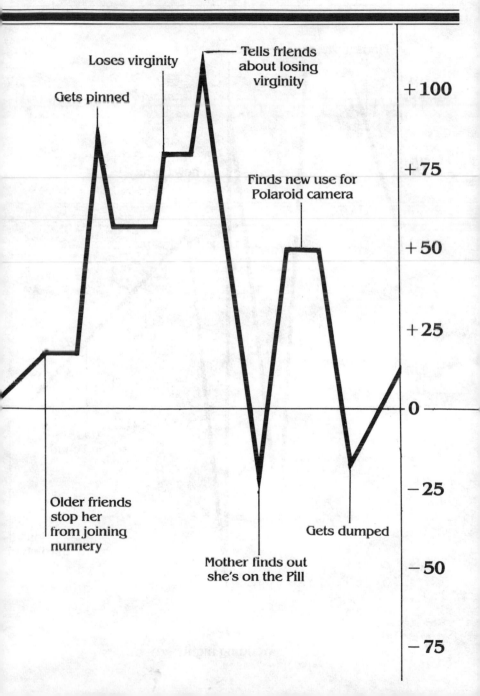

Loses virginity

Tells friends about losing virginity

Gets pinned

Finds new use for Polaroid camera

+100

+75

+50

+25

0

Older friends stop her from joining nunnery

Mother finds out she's on the Pill

Gets dumped

−25

−50

−75

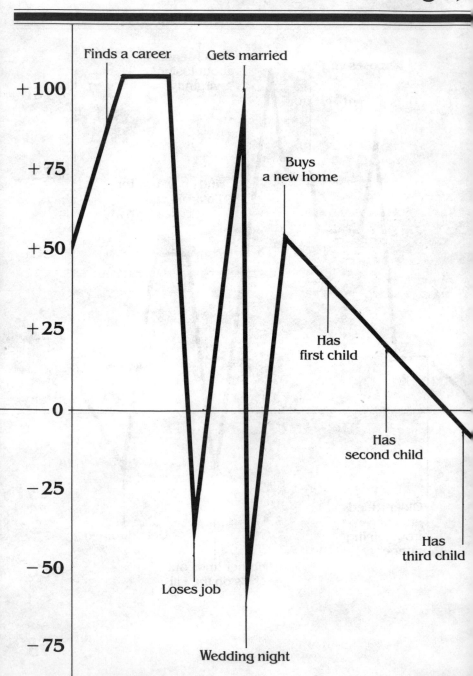

Finds a career

Gets married

Buys a new home

+ 100

+ 75

+ 50

+ 25

0

− 25

− 50

− 75

Has first child

Has second child

Has third child

Loses job

Wedding night

Sexual Satisfaction (Continued)

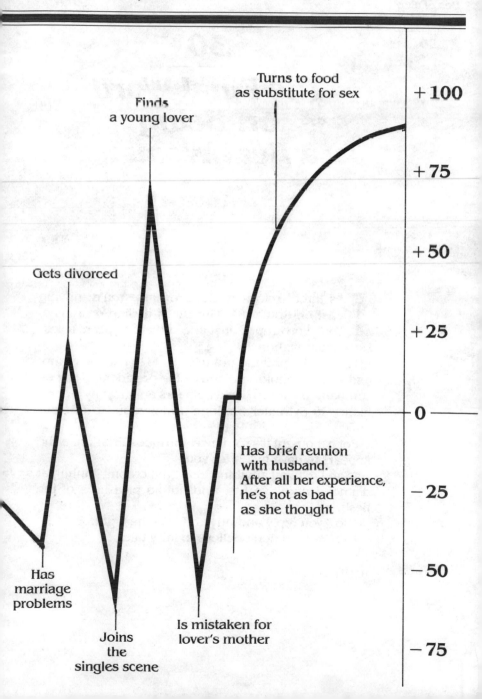

Turns to food as substitute for sex

Finds a young lover

Gets divorced

Has marriage problems

Joins the singles scene

Is mistaken for lover's mother

Has brief reunion with husband. After all her experience, he's not as bad as she thought

+100

+75

+50

+25

0

−25

−50

−75

30

*The Final Word
on Being
a Real Woman*

It's three o'clock in the morning. You're driving east on Route 40. The car is gliding on fumes. You're on empty. Just ahead there appears a self-service gas station.

You pull in, pretend not to be able to use the pump, and lo and behold, the son of the president of the oil company, a young man who bears an uncanny resemblance to Sylvester Stallone, ambles out to fill your tank.

For a moment it's romance, intrigue, flirtation, as he appears to have fallen for you.

"Can I get you anything else?" he croons, hinting at diamond rings, yachts, and untold pleasures of the flesh.

"No," you reply and drive off into the night.

Real Women don't believe in fairy tales.